What To Do When You Get That Job Interview

by
Mildred Rivers

CCB Publishing
British Columbia, Canada

What To Do When You Get That Job Interview

Copyright ©2008 by Mildred Rivers
ISBN-13   978-0-9810246-7-7
Second Edition

Library and Archives Canada Cataloguing in Publication

Rivers, Mildred, 1949-
What To Do When You Get That Job Interview / written by Mildred Rivers. – 2nd ed.
ISBN 978-0-9810246-7-7
1. Employment interviewing. I. Title.
HF5549.5.I6R59 2008   650.14'4   C2008-904627-7

This manual is copyrighted by Mildred Rivers with all rights reserved. For information contact: Mildred Rivers, P.O. Box 245, Elmwood Park, NJ, 07047.

Extreme care has been taken to ensure that all information presented in this book is accurate and up to date at the time of publishing. Neither the author nor the publisher can be held responsible for any errors or omissions. Additionally, neither is any liability assumed for damages resulting from the use of the information contained herein.

All rights reserved. No part of this publication may be reproduced, stored in a retrieval system or transmitted in any form or by any means, electronic, mechanical, photocopying, recording or otherwise without the express written permission of the publisher. Printed in the United States of America and the United Kingdom.

Publisher: CCB Publishing
             British Columbia, Canada
             www.ccbpublishing.com

Dedication

*In memory of my parents,
William and Agnes Rivers,
who taught me the importance
of survival and independence.
You are with me in my
thoughts each day.*

ACKNOWLEDGEMENTS

My daughter Celeste, who means the world to me.

My sister Elnora Thomas and her family, for all their love and kindness.

My best friends Evelyn and Ronnie Desciora for their love and friendship and being supportive in everything that I've been involved with.

Contents

What To Do When You Get That Job Interview 1
Interviewer's Questions 3
Interview's Questions For Management Positions 24
Reference Questions Asked By An Interviewer 33
Questions To Ask Of The Interviewer 34

WHAT TO DO WHEN YOU GET THAT JOB INTERVIEW

Before the interview, compile a list of honorable job intentions. Know who and what you are about. This is very important, since we often tend to accept the first job or position offered to us without considering if it is what we want to do or not. Ask yourself these questions such as. Do I work well with others? Do I prefer to work alone? Am I comfortable with regular working hours? Can I handle overtime, and weekends? Whatever the answers are, see yourself in the answers.

Be prepared by gathering as much knowledge as possible about the interviewing company. Go to the library and do some research. Look for information on the company. The Thomas Register, published by Thomas Publishing, One Penn Plaza, New York N. Y. 10001. This reference book is a multi volume work, that shows products and services, company profile and a catalog file for all manufacturers listed. Here you can find out how long the company has been in business, who are its owners or owner, and what have the gross sales, and profit or losses been during the last five years up until now.

What is the growth plan? Get a copy of the annual report. Find out if the company is downsizing or expanding or restructuring. You will be very distraught if you find out after taking the job, that the company is laying off staff, or is being sold or has gone bankrupt. Review what you have done on previous jobs. Make a list of the good, bad, and indifferent.

What To Do When You Get That Job Interview

INTERVIEWER'S QUESTIONS

The questions that are listed are for you to go over and over again. These questions are the most asked questions by the interviewer.

1. According to your qualifications, have you done the best work you are capable of doing? (Pick out your best work and be brief.)

_____
_____
_____
_____
_____
_____
_____

2. What have you learned from your previous jobs? (Be positive and brief.)

_____
_____
_____
_____
_____
_____
_____

3. Which of your jobs was the least interesting? Why? (Never say anything bad about your previous employers.)

_____
_____
_____
_____
_____
_____

4. What kind of employee are you? (Be truthful.)

_____
_____
_____
_____
_____
_____

5. On your last performance evaluation, what did your supervisor criticize you for? (Give a minor example if you have one.)

_____
_____
_____
_____
_____
_____

6. How do you normally handle criticism? (Give an example, for instance, from suppliers, from peers, or co workers, or from customers and clients.)

_____
_____
_____
_____
_____
_____

7. What are your weaknesses? (With regards to work skills.)

_____
_____
_____
_____
_____
_____

8. What have you done to correct those weaknesses? (Give one good example.)

_____
_____
_____
_____
_____
_____

9. How do you normally handle failure? (Be brief.)

_____
_____
_____
_____
_____
_____

10. What are you looking for in your next job? (Be brief mention improvement.)

_____
_____
_____
_____
_____
_____

11. Have you ever been terminated or asked to resign? Why? (If yes or no, be vague.)

_____
_____
_____
_____
_____
_____

12. Why have you held so many jobs? (Talk about your needs.)

___

13. Why did you stay with one company so long? (An example is security.)

___

14. Do you consider yourself a loyal employee? (Yes, no elaboration.)

___

15. What are your career goals/objectives? (Be brief and job associated.)

_____
_____
_____
_____
_____
_____

16. How does this job fit in with your career goals? (Talk about goals and financial directive.)

_____
_____
_____
_____
_____
_____

17. How do you feel about further training? (Always give positive answers.)

_____
_____
_____
_____
_____
_____

18. How do you normally handle changes on the job? (Be positive.)

_____
_____
_____
_____
_____
_____
_____

19. Would you like to have your boss's job? (Use tact when you answer this one.)

_____
_____
_____
_____
_____
_____
_____

20. Why haven't you progressed more in your career? (Example, convenience.)

_____
_____
_____
_____
_____
_____
_____

What To Do When You Get That Job Interview

21. Have you ever been turned down for a raise? (Always say no.)

_____
_____
_____
_____
_____
_____
_____

22. Why aren't you earning more money at your age? (Leave out feminist and racial tones.)

_____
_____
_____
_____
_____
_____
_____

23. Do you consider yourself promotable? (Always say yes and have an explanation.)

_____
_____
_____
_____
_____
_____
_____

24. What is the hardest thing you ever had to do in your job? (Be brief.)

_____
_____
_____
_____
_____
_____

25. How would you describe your boss's style? (Give positive answers.)

_____
_____
_____
_____
_____
_____

26. How would you describe your relationship with your boss? (Give positive answers.)

_____
_____
_____
_____
_____
_____

27. What have you learned from your boss? (Be positive.)

___

28. Have you ever been caught up in office politics before? (If you answer yes, be prepared to give an example.)

___

29. Do you prefer to work alone or with others? (Say both and explain.)

___

30. Do you consider yourself a team player? (Say yes and explain.)

31. Do you consider yourself self-motivated? (Describe a time when you took the initiative to accomplish something.)

32. Could you give me three personal characteristics that best describe you? (Give two or three words only, and be ready to explain them.)

33. What motivates you? (Give positive answers.)

_____
_____
_____
_____
_____
_____

34. What kind of relationship do you have with your peers? (Always use respect.)

_____
_____
_____
_____
_____
_____

35. What kind of people do you prefer to work with? (Be sure to answer with people.)

_____
_____
_____
_____
_____
_____

36. What were the people like at your last company? (Describe good variations.)

_____
_____
_____
_____
_____
_____

37. What did you like least about your last employer? (Be short and positive.)

_____
_____
_____
_____
_____
_____

38. Were you satisfied with your performance at your last company? (Say yes and explain briefly, be positive.)

_____
_____
_____
_____
_____
_____

39. Were they satisfied with you? (Always say yes, but could not account for all.)

_____
_____
_____
_____
_____
_____
_____

40. Why has it taken you so long to find a new job? (Example will be committed to the job.)

_____
_____
_____
_____
_____
_____
_____

41. Why does this job interest you? (Self-explanatory.)

_____
_____
_____
_____
_____
_____
_____

42. What kind of contribution do you think you could make to our organization? (Give positive answers.)

___

43. What part of this job interests you the most? (Be specific.)

___

44. What makes you different from other candidates? (Always state your intelligence and needs.)

___

45. Where would you like to be in 3-5 years? (Never mention your boss's job, because you might not get there. Let company decide.)

_____
_____
_____
_____
_____
_____

46. How do you expect to get there? (Hard work and positive attitude.)

_____
_____
_____
_____
_____
_____

47. What would you do if you detected a peer falsifying expense records? (Never accuse unless your 100% sure.)

_____
_____
_____
_____
_____
_____

48. Give me three areas in which you would like to improve. (Be brief and job related.)

_____
_____
_____
_____
_____

49. Who or what has had the greatest influence on the development of your career interests? (A positive person.)

_____
_____
_____
_____
_____

50. What kind of work do you want to do? (Job related.)

_____
_____
_____
_____
_____

51. What has been your greatest challenge? (Use positive improvements.)

_____
_____
_____
_____
_____
_____

52. Describe a situation where you had a conflict with another individual, and how you dealt with it? (Positive answer and positive dealings.)

_____
_____
_____
_____
_____
_____

53. What interests or concerns you about the position or the company? (Be positive and brief.)

_____
_____
_____
_____
_____
_____

54. What idea have you developed and implemented that was particularly creative or innovative? (Be honest and brief.)

___

55. What characteristics do you think are important for this position? (Be positive and brief.)

___

56. How have your educational and work experiences prepared you for this position? (Be positive and brief.)

___

57. Are you willing to relocate or travel as part of your career? (You should know the answer to this one before they ask you.)

_____
_____
_____
_____
_____
_____

58. Describe a situation where you had to work with someone who was difficult. How was the person difficult, and how did you handle it? (Answer with no disrespect intended.)

_____
_____
_____
_____
_____
_____

59. What frustrates you the most? (Give positive answer and do not elaborate too much.)

_____
_____
_____
_____
_____
_____

60. What else should I know about you? (You should have something positive and important for this answer.)

_____
_____
_____
_____
_____
_____
_____

INTERVIEWER'S QUESTIONS FOR MANAGEMENT POSITIONS

The questions listed, are for supervisors and managers to go over. You should know how to answer these questions like a professional.

1. Beginning with your move into your first supervisory job, would you tell me briefly why each change was made?

_____
_____
_____
_____
_____
_____
_____

2. Referring to your most recent position, what would you say are some of your more important accomplishments?

_____
_____
_____
_____
_____
_____
_____

3. There are always a few negatives about a position. What would you say you liked least about the position?

_____
_____
_____
_____
_____

4. I am interested in how you do your planning. What planning processes have you found useful, and how do you go about them?

_____
_____
_____
_____
_____

5. What are some examples of important types of decisions or recommendations you are called upon to make?

_____
_____
_____
_____
_____

6. What decisions are easiest for you to make and which ones are more difficult?

7. Most of us improve in our decision-making ability as we get greater experience. In what respects do you feel you have improved in your decision making?

8. What has been your experience with major expansion or reduction of force?

9. How many immediate subordinates have you removed from their jobs in the last few years? Any contemplated?

10. How many immediate subordinates have you promoted in the past two years? How did you go about it? Any surprises or disappointments?

11. Some managers keep a very close check on their staff. Others use a loose rein. What pattern do you follow? How has it changed in the last few years?

12. Sometimes it is necessary to issue direct authority to an individual or the entire staff. Do you have any recent examples of direct authority that you have issued?

_____
_____
_____
_____
_____
_____
_____

13. What do you think contributes to your effectiveness as a supervisor?

_____
_____
_____
_____
_____
_____
_____

14. What kind of supervisor gets the best performance out of you?

_____
_____
_____
_____
_____
_____
_____

15. Some managers are quite deliberate about such things as communications, development, and motivation. Do you have any examples of how you do this?

_____
_____
_____
_____
_____
_____

16. How do you feel about your progress (career-wise) to date?

_____
_____
_____
_____
_____
_____

17. What would you do if the company you had joined gave you $2,000 to spend during the first year any way you felt appropriate? (Key word appropriate, mention relocation or office supplies.)

_____
_____
_____
_____
_____
_____

18. When you terminate somebody, other than severing them from the company, what would be your key objective? Why? (Example, poor work habits or always tardy)

_____
_____
_____
_____
_____
_____

19. What benefits can be expected from pushing an employee to do better? When would you do that?

_____
_____
_____
_____
_____
_____

20. When you are supervising people, how do you motivate them?

_____
_____
_____
_____
_____
_____

21. How do you handle failures or weaknesses in others?

22. What has been the most important surprise you have received from something getting out of control? Why did it happen?

23. What have you done about your own development in the last few years?

24. What characteristics are most important in a good manager?

_____
_____
_____
_____
_____
_____
_____

25. Tell me about a difficult decision you had to make?

_____
_____
_____
_____
_____
_____
_____
_____

REFERENCE QUESTIONS ASKED BY AN INTERVIEWER

1. How long did the applicant work for you?

2. What was the quality of the work?

3. How much responsibility did the applicant have?

4. How did the applicant get along with others?

5. Did the applicant require close supervision?

6. Was the applicant prompt?

7. Why did the applicant leave your company?

8. Do you know of anything that would disqualify the applicant for the job we're considering hiring the applicant for?

9. Can you think of anything I should know about the applicant that I haven't asked about?

10. Do you know anyone else to whom I could speak about the applicant?

QUESTIONS TO ASK OF THE INTERVIEWER

1. What are the duties and responsibilities for this position?

2. How can the job be upgraded?

3. How long has the position been in existence?

4. How long has the position been open?

5. Did he or she succeed or fail?

6. What happens to them?

7. Who are the people's-immediate superior, subordinates, associates in related departments-with whom I will be working?

8. What are their titles, history with the company, previous background, education, etc?

9. Where does this position fit into the company's organization plan?

10. What are the reporting channels?

11. Does the company have an orientation program for new employees?

12. How do I become familiar with company policies, practices, and etiquette?

13. Does the company have an executive development program?

14. If relocating, where can I get information on housing, cost of living, religious, social organizations, shopping, community, schools, libraries, educational and recreational facilities, etc.

15. Does the company offer stock options or deferred payment plans?

16. Does the company reimburse moving expenses? Losses incurred in selling one's house? Living and travel expenses while employee is commuting and finding permanent housing for his/her family?

17. What is the company's policy regarding agency fees?

18. What is the company's policy regarding vacation and sick leave?

19. When and how is the salary usually paid?

20. What are the prospects for salary increase? Promotions?

Well, there you have it, all the information that will help you to relax at your next interview. Remember to get organized, review what you did on your previous jobs, dress professional, don't be cocky, show interest, be on time, show good eye contact, don't be rude or demanding, give good answers, be honest, use good grammar, and know yourself well.

God helps those who help themselves.
Good luck and God bless.

Notes

NOTES

Notes

Notes

www.ingramcontent.com/pod-product-compliance
Lightning Source LLC
Chambersburg PA
CBHW071802040426
42446CB00012B/2676

9780981024677